Outside the Beechwood

by Ellie Buchanan

Illustrations by Lizzy Mikietyn

First published in 2024 by
Bold Wren Press Limited
Edinburgh

www.boldwrenpress.com

This book has been typeset in Cambria Pro by Sharon McTeir
Printed in Cornwall, England

BOLD WREN
PRESS

Part One

Chapter 1

Shocked, Macky let his thoughts scurry away from him like beech-nuts in a blizzard. His heart pounded in his great furry chest – loud and jarring in the sleepy beech wood. It woke the trees that loomed above him, sending their shadowy bodies into an uneasy dance. It caused their leaves to fall and cover the well-trodden path in an untidy carpet of flickering red; while the sound of their rustling was the song of the unknown – vast and ever changing – tauntingly near.

The unknown, well, that was a thing that very seldom strayed with-in the borders of this wood. In fact the Beechwood was the kind of place where everything was well kept, comfortable and quite un-naturally static. It was also the kind of place that none of its sleepy and settled inhabitants ever dreamt of venturing beyond, and that is why Macky – and all the other members of the Macky species – had always lived in that same place, that safe and quiet place in the tamest of beech woods. That is also why – when this young and rather naive Macky now found himself stopped quite sudden-ly, staring at a very odd creature indeed – it had given him a most unexpected shock. A shock that was not only unwelcome, (as often the most useful things are in such beech woods) but also uncom-fortably '*beyond*'... However, more on this later, as for now we must be returning to our friend, Macky, who now, barely able to gather back his thoughts – barely daring to do so, had begun to tentatively sidle down the track; back towards his home, and away from the creature, in the wild hope that it would not notice him go.

However, he had not gone far before he heard from behind him a helpless cry. This was a cry of desperation and hope at once; a cry that thundered with emotion. Like a great mountain torrent, or a bellowing ocean storm, it rushed through the wood. It swirled towards the bewildered Macky, circling about him, enfolding him in its cloud of passion; until soon it had got right under his fur, and right to the centre of his thudding heart. It had a strength to it that Macky had never before felt; for torrents, storms, and such feelings that they held, were things that were of course quite unknown to Macky – they were things that would never have been found in the placid Beechwood. And yet as it throbbed through his heart, it seemed that the cry had sown a small glowing seed of passion and care into the young Macky, and he now found himself stood, as if on a bridge between love and fear... His mind, which was shut as tight as a clamshell, told him urgently to run, but in his heart something had opened, and it seemed that it began to burn all the more, the longer the child wailed...

Time stretched.

Macky turned towards the creature.

He took a step closer.

And another.

He hoped that it would *do* something; move, speak, *anything* to ease the situation: to give him some sort of clue that it was 'normal' and 'expected'. But instead it just sat perfectly still watching him with big teary eyes.

How infuriating.

Slowly he shuffled back towards the creature – for he found that he just could not help it – and pausing for a moment at the place where he had first spotted it; he now took a step closer. But still, it didn't budge.

Time stretched some more.

Eventually Macky could bear the tension no more, and so, summoning up an outrageous amount of bravery he picked the creature off the track with his long fingernails, and held it close to his heart, which was beating at the double.

'This might go down in Macky history!'
He declared through his nervous giggles. In fact, it was actually the start of 'Macky history': the Mackys (a species who all went by the same name in order to inoculate themselves against imagination) had never had a history, as everything they did had always been the same, and because of that they had not much at all to record in the way of stories. They lived amongst the beech trees, doing the same things, in the same places, at the same time, caring not at all for the outside world or any of its inconveniences. In fact they didn't even believe there was an outside world.

The Beechwood was their world. The Beechwood was *the* world. It was all that was predictable because it was all that they knew. They didn't want to know more, or think differently because then they would find that there were things that they *didn't* know, and that *weren't* predictable, and that was quite too much for any Macky.

Yet now as Macky shuffled home, this tiny specimen of the unknown held tightly in his paw, he felt alongside his fear, that feeling that was stronger than any fear – that feeling that had begun to burn in the very centre of his heart.

But Macky had only shuffled a few paces when the voice of the creature presently piped out, stopping him in his tracks: 'excuse me' it said as it looked up at its rescuer (it was looking into a face as soft as a marshmallow with eyes as bland as cheap toast). 'Excuse me, sir, but I've lost my way, and I hoped you could help me get home?'

The bewildered Macky let his thoughts fret and panic for a moment before sifting out of the mess a couple of comprehensible ones.

'Umm that's exactly where I was heading,' he said soothingly. You see to Macky there was only one home – his home; and that was in the centre of the Beechwood.

'I've never heard of anyone getting *lost* before,' he mused. 'But then again I've never seen *you* before either,' he giggled bravely. He was about to ramble on in an attempt to figure out the situation, using Beechwood logic, whilst simultaneously keeping his mind closed as tight as a clamshell. How could there possibly be anything out there if *he* didn't understand it? Yet if he had never even *seen* it, how could he possibly understand it? So that meant that nothing that he had not seen could possibly be there!

Yet here it was!!

His brain whirled round like a stuck record. And he began to grow dizzy with the thought...

' No! You misunderstand!' It interrupted. 'My home is out of this forest, I got lost in the mist you see. I'm not sure how I got here but I'm sure I could direct you to my home once we're out of the woods...'

At that Macky's clamshell brain clamped shut immediately. Don't be absurd. There is nothing outside the Beechwood.
Everyone knew that.

He continued briskly towards his Beechwood house.

On arriving home Macky found his mother right where he knew she'd be – polishing the surface by the door. She always did that at ten past 10.00 am; starting with the cabinet to the left of the door, and working her way round the house clockwise from there...

'Mother!' he yelped, 'I have found an extraordinary creature!'

'Oh.' She said, 'That's nice. Is it a squirrel or a badger?' These were the only other residents of the Beechwood.

Outside the Beechwood

'No mother!' he said in a shrill voice, 'it's a ... um ... it's a ... er ...'

He paused and looked at its smooth velvety skin wrapped in colourful cladding. It didn't really resemble anything in the Beechwood at all, and it certainly did not resemble a Macky. Like Macky, everyone here had furry paws and a perfectly round circumference, long teeth for cracking beechnuts, and short shuffling legs... 'It's a Smoothling!' He exclaimed at last, having opened his clamshell brain wide enough to let a new word slip in.

'No such thing!' his mother said relieved, as she looked into his paws; and saw only the nothing she associated with such nonsense. 'You must be dreaming. No other explanation fits the logic.' 'Or, did you eat a bad mushroom?' She scolded him confidently.

The Smoothling, who was in fact a child, began to cry.

Tears rolled down its plump little cheeks and sunk deep into Macky's paws, leaving an unfamiliar smell similar to damp flowers; and that new feeling that burned in his heart grew and swelled. Macky's mother seemed thoroughly unconcerned and had got back to her work, quite satisfied with her conclusion that Macky was either dreaming or having some sort of reaction to bad food. She didn't believe in 'Smoothlings', there was no such thing as a 'Smoothling'; she couldn't even see the 'Smoothling'. So therefore it wasn't there.

Macky however, stood by the door a good while longer. For although he yearned so very deeply for the warmth and comfort of his home on this most uncomfortable and unusual day, he found that he could

not leave the threshold. For his mind whirled round in chaos – part of it telling him that his mother was right, and part of it telling him that his heart was right, and though he had never even liked the game much, he now felt as though he was playing a particularly competitive game of tug of war with himself.

For the thing is, that once a clamshell brain has been even ever so slightly pried open – no matter how hard it shuts itself again – there are always new feelings and thoughts that have snuck in, which one cannot understand fully, yet understands enough to know that they are there – quite an infuriating state of mind for one such as Macky. The other problem is that once it has been opened once, its seal is never quite as strong and may have the terrifying tendency to do so again.

The longer the child cried, the more it tugged at Macky's heart. And the longer those new and difficult-to-grasp feelings flitted about him, the more restless he became. And so it was that Macky agreed to take the Smoothling home; and that indeed was the bravest thing that any Macky had ever yet achieved.

Chapter 2

At the time Macky was still confidently convinced that there *was* nothing other than the Beechwood; and therefore this *Smoothling* must come from some obscure treetop where even squirrels never went. Or a burrow, in which it had hid for so long that it had never needed to develop fur... Either that or they would reach the edge of the wood and the Smoothling would be content to be left in the nothingness outside, which it was eccentric enough to call its home.

But as their journey progressed, and the beech trees grew thinner and ever more crooked and sparse, Macky began to feel less and less sure of these ideas – while the child, became more and more confident of *his* ideas, and as he rode on Macky's broad shoulders he shouted out in excitement, 'Home! Home! Home! Home!!! We must be near the edge of the forest by now! Then we'll reach the moors of Mulach!'

Macky didn't know what a moor was, or a Mulach but he wasn't about to learn something *new*, especially not from a *Smoothling* only the size of his paw.

'Now, now' said Macky, mustering as much of a responsible tone as he could under the pressing circumstances. 'Are you sure you want me to leave you out in that nothing? You'll be all alone!' he said, suddenly trembling like a buttercup in a blizzard. You see, he had grown really very fond of the little Smoothling and was now reluctant to let it go. But the Smoothling took no notice of Macky's cluttering fears and doubts – such was its strength and courage – and so their journey continued.

Now the Beechwood isn't much bigger than a regular country park – and traveling by its well-kept paths only takes a few

Beechwood hours to cross, so that soon the edge of the Beechwood had reached them and the familiar signpost marked:

'THE END'

Stood a paws length away. Beyond it, was…

Nothing.

Empty space, that had the smell of cold hostility and a wildness that was quite revolting to any Macky.

As he stood in front of 'The End' sign Macky felt his paws begin to tremble; then his knees, then his arms, till soon his whole body was sent into an uncontrollable shiver. Macky had seen 'The End' sign many times before, but this time something was different. It was as though there had once been a wall that had stood, somewhere, in his mind somewhere on this frail border between Beechwood and beyond – that blocked what lay outside the wood. But the wall had now begun to tumble down, and although Macky really knew nothing of walls or Beechwoods, or what lay beyond them, it sent a queer feeling creeping into him then… He wanted to shut his eyes, but they would only grow wider – he wanted to turn for home, but his feet were rooted to the ground… And yet amidst his fear Macky noticed that a little beam of light was filtering in; it was the laughter of the child, which crept into Macky's awareness; for the child meanwhile, oblivious to Macky's fears, was shrieking with joy. 'The moors the moors!' It yelped taking deep breaths as if it hadn't breathed since it had entered the Beechwood, while letting its sweet careless laughter ring through the air – that very same laughter that knocked the wall down, between Beechwood and beyond.

Like dew drops, this laughter began to melt Macky's fear, but as it did he noticed all of a sudden that the Smoothling had slid from his back and waddled out past 'THE END' sign. And to his surprise Macky felt himself quite impulsively reaching out to snatch it back.

But the Smoothling refused to return. 'Come on!' It said, 'there's still a long way to go, I come all the way from the mountains, miles away from here!' Macky was now beginning to get overwhelmed, but just as he went to protest to the Smoothling's plan, he suddenly realized that he had moved out of the Beechwood himself!!

And now all he saw around him was, well...

Nothing.

Suddenly he knew how it was to be lost.

'I'm lost.'

Said Macky in a defeated voice, as panic and despair rose within him.

'No, no! The mist has cleared!?' came the Smoothling's voice as though from a distance –

'I know the way from here, we only have to follow the burn up through that meadow, and we'll be on our way,' said the restless and perplexed Smoothling.

The burn bubbled excitedly down from the moors carrying the fresh smell of crystalized light. The meadow was one of lofty tussocks, which amused themselves in the wind.

Macky however, saw none of these things.

He saw nothing.

His pride had begun to dissolve rapidly since he had left the wood, and his clamshell brain felt as though it had begun to disintegrate in the nothing, which surrounded him. Suddenly all his emotions came at once.

He sat down in the nothing like a helpless beechnut stranded in a puddle.

It was the child who now took pity.

'*Please* help me!'

It begged. 'I *can't* return home on my own. I need your strong legs to carry me, and your warm fur to sleep in.'

'And it's lonely on the moors' It added. 'But not with company...'

This comforted Macky. He felt strength seeping up him from his sturdy legs and warmth creeping through him from his long thick fur. He looked at the Smoothling. It looked vulnerable and was quivering like an autumn leaf despite its courage; and it was at that moment that Macky felt his fear begin ever so slightly to evaporate and, in its place, the very beginnings of a courageous warmth and certainty had begun to take seed inside him. He was out of the Beechwood, and the unknown lay all about him. New things could grow here; change was dancing in the air. He lifted the Smoothling onto his shoulders.

And so their adventure outside the Beechwood began.

Chapter 3

Time had disappeared for Macky. There was nothing to measure it against, now that the familiar shadows of the beech trees no longer ticked like clocks. Space had gone too, naturally, since they were now in nothing. Macky tried not to think of that too much, it made his clamshell brain feel more like a quivering flower in spring. He didn't like feeling all fragile and dainty.

The Smoothling guided him with remarkable patience. 'Follow the river!' it chirped.

Eventually Macky had had to admit that he could see no river, and it must therefore be in the child's imagination. He thought back fondly to his own early childhood, when *he* had had an imagination. He used to make up stories for the squirrels, he had tried with the badgers too, but their tempers were easily stirred... However his imagination was curbed, when his mother discovered him talking to a squirrel, and she had taken him to see Doctor Droon, who had been most perplexed, and tried to stamp out this strangeness.

'Then follow the sound of it!' the Smoothling urged.

At first Macky could hear nothing, but thinking back to his childhood had taken his mind off the fact that they were in 'nothing', and he soon found himself forgetting many other Beechwood ideas as well; ideas that had not been with him when he was very young, but had begun to cling to him through life – like limpets that grew very fast, and that had caused his ears to grow rather subjective. But now as these ideas began to disintegrate (for he was no longer in the right climate for them to grow) Macky presently began to hear the rushing, bubbling noise of water. It was much more lively than the stream in the Beechwood, but still unmistakably a river!

He followed it gladly. It was such a comfort to have around in this nothing!

As time went on they started to feel hungry.
The Smoothling collected berries and Macky had brought a beechnut bannock, which they shared between them. At first Macky refused the berries, 'they weren't like anything in the Beechwood,' he grumbled. But after polishing of his portion of the bannock he gave in.

They tasted stronger than Macky's own legs and were even more of a comfort than his fur...

Just then his meandering train of thoughts came to a sudden and snappish halt.
He had *seen* them!

He could *feel* them, and taste them, and throw them in the direction of the burn, which bubbled as excitedly as he did!

The terrifying nothingness, which had surrounded him, was now rapidly beginning to disappear and he realized it had in fact only been in his ... well... imagination he supposed. It was not so empty, and not so nothing.

The river laughed by them, and the moors hosted tussocks of windswept grass and low-growing bushes of purple berries, which frolicked and danced merrily in the breeze.

Slowly, Macky began to see his surroundings as a world that was different from his own, yet so similar compared to the nothing he had been in before. It hung about him, vast and alive, filling his vision with such clarity that it made the world of the Beechwood seem like its reflection in a vague and murky puddle.

Slowly as the days went on and their journey continued, the child taught Macky the ways of the moors. The edible plants, the ways to hide from the hurrying wind. The things the light can tell you, and the clouds. Macky found himself listening to the Smoothling with a newfound respect and wonder, no longer with pride, and an air of pompous and naive arrogance. He also found that the frail spring flower that his clamshell-brain had become had grown somewhat sturdier and happier, flourishing in the wonders of the newness, embracing it, and bursting into a full summer bloom. No more did he hide in fear of what he did not know. No longer did he grumble and reminisce that the Beechwood was 'Oh so much better than any other place.' And as they proceeded, the rounded moors grew larger in their confidence, and the shrubs smaller in their needlessness.

Now that Macky had settled quite a bit and had even begun to enjoy the newness inside him and around him, he had almost forgotten all the rules and ways of the Beechwood. In fact, the place had started to seem really quite odd to him, (although he would still never admit that to the Smoothling!) It was not really the kind of place a flower could ever bloom in full, to put it kindly. For although beech trees are wonderful, and certainly to be appreciated, it is far from wonderful to live in a beech wood that you think is the *whole* world. For without its context it soon grows to seem altogether different from an *actual* beech wood.

So with this newfound appreciation Macky had begun to think less and less about himself and his troubles, and notice more and more about the world around him – the moors, the clouds, and the Smoothling.

Now one morning it dawned on the ever-strengthening Macky that he had no idea how the Smoothling had got all the way from his city (which was still not in sight) to the Beechwood. It felt like they had been traveling forever and the child had even grown, so that Macky had had to make new clothes for him out of his excess winter fur.

When Macky posed the question to the Smoothling, the boy replied 'I don't rightly know', feeling uncertain. 'My home is called Scurr Mór, and it is the gateway town to the mountains, I had been with my father out fishing in a loch about a day's walk from home. The memories are blurry.' He said shaking his head. 'We went out in the boat my father kept there, but then the weather turned bad and the loch grew wild. The boat began to rock, and I remember getting swept out of the boat and into the loch. I don't remember much after that, until I woke up beached on the moors. It was all misty and while looking for something to eat I lost the river and stumbled into that queer forest you found me in.'

Macky thought of the child floating helplessly down the stream, and began to cry. He wondered what had happened to the Smoothling's father. The child wondered too, but neither of them spoke of it; though they both knew what the other was thinking. They had become quite close to one another by this point and quite often the child would know what Macky was going to say even before he did, and vice versa.

Now the ground had become much steeper as moor gave way to scree; dotted here and there with delicate golden ferns, which reminded Macky of his fond fatherly feelings towards the Smoothling. Large slopes rose around them with daunting cliffs, which taunted them with an air of cool indifference. The river had been getting thinner and more frantic, and although they followed it as best they could, sometimes it would disappear into a narrow and terrifying-looking ravine.

Now they scrambled alongside it, and as the Smoothling clambered nimbly among the rocks, Macky pottered on behind, staring in awe at the ferocity of the river and wondering how on earth something so vulnerable-looking as the Smoothling could have been swept all the way down it and survived; and it seemed to Macky then that the world itself was such a river, and life – the fragility of the Smoothling. Yet somehow, there was something, that kept it afloat...

Suddenly a great roaring drowned out Macky's thoughts. He looked up, and was startled to see that a wall of simply impassable rock lay in front of them – and down it tumbled the water, like a white smoky dragon, which spat with power and life.

The Smoothling turned round and glanced at Macky's short stubby legs, which were about as flexible as Macky's mother's thoughts. 'Surely it wasn't expecting him to climb that!?' Macky fretted.

The Smoothling sighed worriedly.

Slowly a realisation came to Macky. He could not go on. And even for the Smoothling it would be dangerous. He did not want to let the Smoothling go on, but the look on the Smoothling's face was no

longer that of the helpless child he had found in the Beechwood; but rather one of a growing hero who had travelled the globe and learnt much about himself and the world. There was also a look of deep sorrow. He had grown to love Macky and saw Macky's own love for him in his big brown eyes which were no longer so bland at all, but rather twinkling and alive. But he knew that Macky could not make it. He also knew that he had to return to his people again. They both knew. These thoughts passed between them without words, as they had now so often come to do.

Chapter 4

They slept one more night together on a patch of tepid moss next to the waterfall. As they fell asleep they stared at the stars and the watery dragon's smoke, which drifted from the relentless beast – who neither guarded them nor troubled them.

It was on some mission of its own, blowing day into night, and the easy flow of time into fragments, which would do as they wished.

These thoughts crept into the sleepers' minds and an idea struck them then that perhaps they too could let their time do as they wished – letting the time they had spent together grow so big that it could seem ever present in all the future time that was to come.

The Smoothling climbed the cliff through clouds of doubtful thoughts and feelings, which threw him off at every step, until his climbing felt more like the shaky scrabbling of a stuck beetle.

But from below came the comforting voice of Macky:

'Focus on every step at a time,' he said wisely, 'and remember that the world is much too full of 'What Ifs' – and whatever happens *they* mustn't be allowed to decide the turn of events!' This comforted the Smoothling and he finished the climb quite bravely.When he reached the summit of the cliff he saw what he had truly hoped to see the loch, and beyond it, nestled between the looming mountains – his city, his people, his home. And so he hurried on.

The Smoothling had promised to return to visit Macky once he had seen his family. He promised he would bring them with him, and that they would help him haul Macky up the cliff to his home.

But the truth to be told was that although Macky loved the Smoothling so very very much, he was quite glad to be left in his newfound home amongst the wild mountains and heathery moors – away from the busyness of the city of Smoothlings. Yes, this was his place for now, here in the wilds by the dragon. It held a wisdom and sturdy presence that he took comfort in. He took comfort too in the rocks, which gaped at him with quirky expressions, and the golden ferns which reminded him of the flourishing of his mind and

heart. He never felt alone here, and of course the company of the Smoothling never left him either. Their hearts were always together – for distance does not weaken the voice of the heart.

When at last the Smoothling's people did come to help haul Macky up the cliff, as the Smoothling had wished, they could not even see Macky.

They said there was no such thing as a 'Macky', and that the Smoothling was daydreaming.

They never returned. But Macky wasn't resentful. He had not forgotten how it felt to be so scared and closed minded that you saw and knew so very, very little. He had not forgotten that once he had not been able to see much more than beech trees and badgers.

Of course, the Smoothling returned to visit Macky many a time after that, making sure to bring with him the children of the Smoothling town (and before too long his own little children too!) to play and listen to stories with Macky. Making sure they saw him at an early age so that they never lost their sight of the unordinary, or let their minds become narrowed.

Part Two

Chapter 5

Time passed in the world of the Smoothlings, largely unheeded, as the years rolled by like a calm ocean swell under a sunset. But as they continued to roll, the swells got steeper and wilder, and a wind picked up. Change was coming, as it always does, but like summer turning to autumn some changes come in an unwelcome guise – though often the best sort of changes do.

And so it was, that as time went on the Smoothling could be found more and more often out in the wilds with Macky and the children, than in his own town, amongst the other adult Smoothlings. For you see, after spending a good deal of time back at home, it had begun to seem ever more to the Smoothling that there was something troubling wafting through the city. And as time went on this *something* that was troubling the Smoothling began to grow on his mind ever more, the longer he did nothing about it.

It held about it the heavy whiff of a something that *was not right* – perhaps even carrying the worrying and unsavoury tinge of *enchantment.*

For since the Smoothling had returned from his adventures with Macky, it had seemed ever more to him, that the people looked upon the world under some sort of queer delusion – perhaps even a spell. The first of the worrying signs had been when his people, even his own father, had not been able to see Macky – but as time went on the Smoothling had noticed all the more signs of this enchantment. It seemed to him that the people were sad and serious, and so terribly afraid. They would never admit this of course, not even to themselves, which only made it worse, so that soon it had become a fear that they never came face to face with, but rather it loitered about them, just out of sight, always offering them an escape from catching sight of its danger, but an escape that left them less brave and more comfortable.

'What has changed here since I've been away?'
'Where is this enchantment coming from?'
'Who is the enchanter?'

The Smoothling wondered.
And as the days rolled on, the Smoothling could be heard muttering more and more of the troubles that grew on his mind as he wandered through the more forgotten parts of the town searching for the enchanter who had cast such a spell.

And as he watched the streets bustle by, no one watched him back. Despite the troubled and sad look on his face, his friends and comrades knew or noticed nothing of his troubled mind, for it seemed that they were caught too deep in their own troubles to notice such things of the outside world. They marched briskly through the streets with placid smiles pasted to their fearful faces. Their heads were bowed to their knees under the weight of their own thoughts, which danced aloft in victory – their masters unable to tame them – they pranced a riot.

Macky would have noticed, thought the Smoothling sadly...

Macky would know what to do, he thought again. The Smoothling hadn't told Macky his trouble yet because he didn't want to worry the old creature. Macky was coming up for 154 years old (though he still showed no actual signs of age, apart from perhaps a little more wisdom and joviality). But now the Smoothling remembered that Macky had always said that asking for help was a very brave and important thing to do and that if the Smoothling wanted to be a true hero he must be very, very brave.

Macky would be out there in the wilds now, thought the Smoothling wistfully, playing with the children in the sunlit spray of the waterfall. He closed his eyes to the dour streets and brought their image to mind: a beautiful sunny image framed by a fresh spring breeze.

What has happened to me, thought the Smoothling with a tired smile, why do I not play in the wilds like the children anymore? For that is where all my true wisdom came from.

Macky was wise and the Smoothling was worried.

The Smoothling would go and find Macky.

Chapter 6

Macky was sitting as usual on his favourite patch of moss next to the waterfall. It was a peaceful spring day and a silent mist had settled close to the ground – a warm blanket over the earth and her creatures.

The Smoothling children frolicked carefree in the quilt of moss and bog cotton that lay underfoot, jumping every now and then into Macky's thick fur. Today the Smoothling's own two children, Vincent and Es, were the only ones who had come to play, these days they spent many such afternoons with Macky. They loved their time with him! He would play with them all day long, and he didn't care a wink as to what people thought of him and his giddy ways. He would let his sunny, kind laughter ring through the air, like an everlasting spring. It was like the music of bells, under-toned by some deep symphony of care, understanding, and wisdom; caught through many treacherous wondering – and days spent in laughter and love despite their toils.

Macky and the two Smoothling children were playing I Spy Cloud: a game in which one looks for creatures and obscure shapes drifting by in the sky. It was the perfect day for it in fact, for a wind had picked up, and all the clouds seemed to be hurrying by at quite a pace, dancing and shifting their shapes as they went. They were on some wild adventure of their own no doubt, thought Macky wistfully.

'You see adventures are something which come and go just when you're needing them; whether you know it or not,' he explained to the children.

'We want an adventure!!' Cried the children at once.

You see they had heard a great deal about adventures from

Macky's many stories, which came to life in them, as though they had been in them themselves. For Macky was a great storyteller, and that is why the children now felt quite prepared for an adventure, and indeed considered themselves professionals in the field: during their many days spent in the wilds with Macky, they would soar with the birds over the mountains, and dance with the bobbing bog cotton in the meadows, which was to them the stars of the night sky brought to earth in many tiny balls of fog.

And so that is how the children had come to know nature and adventures so very well. And while the adults knew a great many names and weights and quantities of the things found in the wilds, the children knew the things themselves.

Vincent and Es were now the same age as the Smoothling had been when he had first set off for his adventures with Macky. Macky watched them fondly as he thought back on that first time he had met a little Smoothling; shivering in the shadows of the Beechwood, all bundled up in colourful cladding, with smooth velvety skin. They were a charming species he thought, albeit a little perplexing. But Macky was glad as he watched the Smoothling children, because they didn't want to be anything other than themselves. Their missions and dreams uplifted and motivated them; and weights upon their shoulders were a faraway thing. Most comforting of all, they could see right through the fragile outer shell of a person, right through to the real person inside. This was how a Smoothling thrived.

When the Smoothling had finally reached them, the moon was high in the sky and the children were fast asleep, contentedly curled in Macky's thick fur. Macky's eyes were closed but he was still awake.

Now at last the Smoothling told Macky his worries.

But Macky didn't seem worried at all.

In fact, on the contrary, he seemed extremely delighted that the Smoothling had noticed the enchantment.

'It's always better not to be blind, even if what you see is difficult.'

He comforted the Smoothling, who had already begun to cheer up.

'You need another adventure, that's what you need!' He continued enthusiastically.

'You'll dig yourself a hole soon, if you carry on stamping the same dreary habits and routines in any longer.'

'You need to feel the wind in your face washing away the whiff of enchantment, and I'll tell you what else you need: you need to climb to the top of the world! That's where you'll find the answer. It's at the top of the world where you'll be able to see it all clearly. Because nothing can hide from the top of the world.'

So, the Smoothling left his children, who were eager to be in the care of their good friend Macky, and set off to find the highest point in the world; Macky had a way of inspiring such zest in him that for the moment his worries were beginning to fade.

Now the children were especially delighted with the plan when Macky said, as soon as the Smoothling had departed, 'Well children, I think this will be a perfect opportunity for our own little adventure what do you think??'

The children shrieked with joy and began to prance, their bounce given extra spring from the purpling heather that they stomped upon.

The Smoothling meanwhile thought of his little children playing innocently under the vigilant care of the old, wise Macky.

'At least they will be safe while I venture into these treacherous lands,' he thought.

But luckily Macky was wise enough to know that children get to an age where they *need* adventure to stop them from growing too much like marshmallows, or cheap toast before it has been toasted, like he himself had done.

A wasted childhood he sometimes used to think, but he had since found out that it's never too late to have a happy childhood!

Now as I'm sure you can imagine this merry company weren't at all long in setting off, for they had no plan at all to slow them down. And soon the roaring of the waterfall was a distant hissing, almost drowned out completely by the silence they had drifted into.

Chapter 7

The two children galloped down the moor, following the river in hurried pursuit. They were bursting at the seams with excitement, and, most of the 'Jammy Pieces' that the Smoothling had packed them to last the next few days.

The river seemed to know well where it was going and the children followed it with merry confidence. Macky bumbled on behind – he walked at a mellow pace on his short shuffling legs.

At last they came to the place where the river opened up like a great mouth, that poured out all its excitement into a quiet open valley. Behind it, the mountain range dwindled away on either side like jagged teeth gnashing at the sky. Macky had come up this way with the Smoothling long ago, and many a time since, but even so it seemed new to him every time, for he had found that nature always had something new to show, and as his mind changed so did the world it saw.

Now Macky felt just as excited as the children, for out in front of him the world opened up to a great dome of moor and sky and he bounded as much as his spring-less legs allowed him to – out towards the welcoming ark of the unknown, where a meadow guarded by mossy hummocks squinted against the golden autumn sun.

Vince and Es were still galloping on ahead with all the bounce of springtime shoots, and they were specks in the distance by now, to Macky. But he wasn't worried about that sort of thing, he knew that they would soon tire and need to curl up in his warm fur.

The sun was beginning to set, and the sky was a fiery red when Macky heard the delighted shrieks of the children who were finally close enough to hear.

'They've stopped!' he concluded.

'And well, that's a relief, I don't think I could have followed them for much longer at that jolly pace,' he muttered to himself.

But from the sound of their voices it didn't seem at all like they had stopped out of exhaustion. 'No' Macky said to himself ruefully. 'They must have found something queer, or interesting – and most likely both at once.'

'The adventure has begun,' he declared to himself.

And he quickened his pace, for he knew that with any adventure it is not long after it begins that one decides they have had enough. And that is exactly when the *real* adventure starts.

At last a heavily panting Macky rounded the last bend in the river and found that the children had indeed found something interesting and queer at once. There, in the last of the crags before the mountains led down to the quieter moors below, was the gaping mouth of a cave. The children couldn't be seen for the darkness, but from inside the cave some echoey giggles could be heard: the Smoothling children weren't very good at hiding, even in the dark. And it was, very dark inside. It took a while for Macky's eyes to adjust enough to be able to see the children, but when he could, he found that they were in a large cavern, and there was no sign of bears.

'Good' said Macky, 'I say we spend the night here before exploring further tomorrow.' The children seemed glad of his choice, and almost before he had finished talking they were nestled up in his fur purring with bliss.

You see they had been waiting a good wee while for Macky to arrive, since their initial discovery, and it seemed that as they had waited tiredness had caught up with them before Macky had...

Chapter 8

Meanwhile, the Smoothling wandered through the cobbled streets of the city, unseen. The moon was big and silver, and reflected itself in the thousands of early morning dewdrops that lined the cobbles like a quilt of stars. He had neared the lesser-known edges of the town and now tiptoed tentatively by, his feet barely tapping the floor. His fingers trembled like white minnows in the moonshine. Before turning every corner, he poked his head round the stark-edged buildings so that only the tip of his nose could be seen from the view of the suspected street. His ears were strained in the hope of catching the sound of wicked spells spiraling down from some unnoticed tower. His heart beat against his chest like a marching band – and despite his quiet footfall *that* sound could have given him away to any enchanter. He jumped at every noise, which seemed to carry especially far in the thick mist that had descended just in time for his adventure. The enchanter could be somewhere very near right now, thought the Smoothling, as his eyes darted wildly through the streets. And in his frenzy every shadow took the form of a looming figure, and every sound was the uttering of a sinister plot...

At last he came to the edge of the city and breathed a sigh – half of relief, and half of disappointment, at having not found the suspected enchantress. For despite what Macky had told him, he had secretly hoped that he would not have to climb all the way to the top of the world to accomplish his mission. But that was of course because he was afraid, and such a mission could never have been accomplished in fear. Now he had searched every single street, having just been through the last; and so there was nothing now for it, but to turn and greet fear with love and bravery. And so the Smoothling took a deep breath, left the town, and headed north.

No one ever went north. North led towards the mountains. Everyone was scared of the mountains, and so the only track he could find was one that had been made by the wild goaty creatures that roamed these parts from time to time. He wandered tentatively along it, his hand trembling a little in his pocket, in which his fist was clenched round nothing in particular, apart from defiance.

Just outside the village there was a small rather battered individual of a tree. It stood alone on the bare shadowed plains, its head held high, its leaves laughing despite its solitude. And it seemed that this tree was the only one brave enough to stand in the shadow of those mountains and greet their howling winds without fear.

It gave the Smoothling great courage that something so fragile had such a strong spirit and joy despite the shadow of the mountain. And now, though he had always looked at the jagged teeth of the mountains and been scared, now the Smoothling felt brave and bold as a knight, and so he walked confidently along the goaty track towards the mountains. His coat shimmered like armour in the moonlight and the mountains loomed at him, imposing and fierce yet not with malice.

The wind howled a ghostly tune.

It grew bitterly cold.

The air was the piercing of a thousand tiny icicles in his throat.

But there are things that always keep one going on, and for the Smoothling love for his people was one of those things. And so, on he went.

He had soon reached the foothills of the mountain and already the enchantment seemed to have eased rapidly. A stark wind met his face in full force, scattering his worries. Bog cotton lined his path like a bed of bobbing stars, which laughed at his passing in their careless bed of purple heather. The Smoothling wandered on, humming gently to keep himself company. Singing always helped at times like this.

The owls hooted.

The light faded.

The day had come and gone.

Creatures scurried in and out of view.

The Smoothling said, 'I wish I had Macky's warm fur to sleep in, I still fancy I could curl up in it now...' And at one point the Smoothling even thought of turning back.

But sometimes in life you simply haven't a choice. If your heart says go, then you simply have to go.

And on he went.

The bog cotton praised his decision with a flurry of movement; then all was still.

Images fluttered through the Smoothling's mind of what he might find when he reached the summit and saw the world and all its ways laid clearly out before him. He was expecting perhaps to see some ghastly beast lurking in the shadows of his own hometown, some menacing enchanter taller than the shadow of the tallest mountain itself... The ground was now steep in front of him and getting steeper. There were no more paths from now on, for the one he had been following faded out feebly a little way in front of him. Even it was not bold enough to climb to the top of the world, thought the Smoothling, as he watched it seeking refuge in the ever thickening bog myrtle shrubs, which grew man high as they thrived on the yellow peaty bog, that squelched between the Smoothlings already sodden toes.

At last the Smoothling arrived at the foot of the tallest mountain that climbed all the way up to the top of the world. It loomed up above him like a great unpassable wave of granite, threatening to crash and roll with all its might on top of him. He stopped and looked at it in awe for a moment, then he carried on up before he could change his mind.

Soon it became clear that despite the Smoothling's tiredness the summit seemed to actually draw him on, for such was his will to get there that nothing at all could bar his way. Indeed its pinpoint peak, ever illusive among the stars, pulled him up like a puppet on a string with its own kind of enchantment. But this, was a much more wholesome sort of enchantment than that which wafted through the town. This enchantment was not thick and heavy – but fresh and crisp, like the winds that tore around him clearing his mind from cobwebs. An enchantment that was so full of life and enthusiasm that he felt that despite the steep climb it was hardly a bother at all to be climbing ever on up – even after a day and a night of walking, for that is how long the Smoothling had now been afoot.

Part Three

Chapter 9

That night, Macky dreamt to the constant drip of a slow-forming stalactite that hung from the cave roof.

He dreamt of frightful beasties and uncomfortable challenges that just kept on coming, and it seemed that the Smoothling was as usual not alone in his unrestful thoughts – for thoughts, being a little like rain – tend to fall on many a mind at once.

When Macky awoke, he was a little shaken, but now suitably prepared for the adventure that was already peeking at him from outside his half-open eyelids. By the time he had got up and done his brief morning stretches he realized that the Smoothling children were no longer clinging to his fur. With a skip and a jump he glanced about him trying not to panic at only the very beginning of the adventure. But just then he heard Vince call out from the darkness that lingered at the back of the cave:

'A passage! I've found a passage!!'

Macky followed his cry hastily; or he thought he followed it – but he couldn't have been sure, because the whole cave now echoed with his words in every direction: 'passage passa pass pa pa...'

When Macky did at last catch up with the children he saw that the passage was narrow, dank and unwelcoming. It seemed to wind on forever, getting gloomier and colder as it went. Perfect! Thought Macky – for they all agreed that this would certainly provide an adventure.

But first of all, to add a little cheer and encouragement to such an adventure, they would be needing a light. It didn't need to be a bright light: in such darkness the full value of even the dimmest of lights is appreciated. It did not even need to be a light that one can see by at all – just something wholesome, just something to warm their hearts; just something to remind them of the sun. Any light of that kind would do.

So Macky went outside to see what he could find. A bright dawn of peach and gold had just broken the horizon, and was now being soaked up into the many flowers that dotted the moors. He picked three small wild roses, sharp smelling, like crystals; white and full of life like the sun, one for each of them. Once he was back in the cave, Macky and the children were pleased to see that the roses still held the best part of the dawn in them, and they were all very much braver for their company. For indeed in such a place the light of encouragement and hope is much more needed than any light that one might simply see by, even though it was very dark inside.

On and on they squeezed and squashed, through the endless winding passage, till time too, began to stretch and squash in such a way that it does in places of that sort. And as they went, their eyes slowly grew more and more accustomed to the underground climate, and their vision began to clear.

But as it did Macky noticed with a fright, that Es had been lagging behind and the faint white glow of her rose was now the size of a dewdrop in the distance.

When Macky arrived at Es he found that she had stopped altogether. 'What's wrong little one?' he asked.

'I'm scared!' said Es.

'No you're not!' said Macky, 'you're Es!'

Macky's company began to warm Es very quickly and his twinkling eyes seemed to find her hidden deep underneath her blanketing fears, and with this reminder she felt herself shining out sturdily from underneath her fear, till she shone so bright that it began to melt her fear altogether. It seemed that Macky had helped her to realize that she *was* Es and only *felt* scared.

It was then that they noticed that Vincent had not stopped with them. In fact, the soft tap taping of his footfall was already so distant that it could almost be mistaken for the dripping of water. Thoughts flashed through Macky's mind of Vincent alone and lost in the darkness; and they set off at once after him.

On they hurried, on and on.

And on.

And on.

The tunnels never ceasing to twist and turn and confront them with new surprises.

Their roses never ceasing to give them strength.

But now they had been going on and on for surely a very long time, and *still* Vincent could neither be seen, nor heard. They called and they called but only the cave answered in long and distant echoes.

Vince wandered on through the darkness with only the thin patter of his feet for company. The others were now far behind, and the soft flip-flopping of Macky's paws could no longer be heard. At first, as he had squirmed through the never-ending passages Vince had been so preoccupied with the task at hand that he had not noticed how far ahead he had got. But when he did at last notice, he had made the terrible mistake of growing suddenly proud. I am so much faster and 'firster' than them! He had said to himself, and so he had sped up all the more.

Now the walls had grown danker and darker around him, and his footsteps more echoey.

This was a place so far from the sun.
An alien world.
The winding guts of the earth.

This was not his home.

'I don't get scared. I'm brave. I'm Vince.'

'Vince is brave.' He repeated, ever more frantically as the tunnel grew darker, and so did his fear. And in this fashion he sped through the tunnel magnifying his danger through such denial of it.

The further Vince went the more alone he felt, and the more he wished for what he missed – for the warmth of Macky and Es's company. For the sun, for the blue sky. He wished for all that was his home – and his heart reached out to these things, and he felt as though he knew them better now than ever, and for a moment, before fear drove their absence to grow larger in his mind than itself, for a moment they were strong in his heart. And that moment was more powerful and everlasting than any fear.

Time stretched till its tricks had lost them entirely, and sometimes Macky and Es felt like they had passed years in this darkness, sometimes only moments. Ever on, ever on they went, and after many more timeless twists in the tunnel there was still no sign of Vince. They began to realize that he wasn't teasing them. They began to get a little more worried. Macky sped up as fast as his short shuffling legs could carry him. Es sunk her hand further into Macky's fur. Macky now became certain that the time had come that they were having a *real* adventure, because at that point they all wanted to turn back.

Chapter 10

Vincent had reached what must have been a larger cavern, from the way it echoed with every breath that he took. He could not see the cavern as he had dropped what little light he had – his rose. He had forgotten its importance in his pride, and now in this absolute darkness, that seemed to have been growing ever heavier around him – he remembered it. He also felt terribly afraid; too afraid to go back for his rose, too afraid even to move. He felt small and shivering and so very alone. More alone than he would have been in the widest ocean. More alone than he would have been on the furthest star; for, overwhelmed by the fear and pride that had been exposed by the darkness (for not all things are covered up by darkness) *he had forgotten himself.* And so he sat down on the damp cave floor and began to cry, and now, as all the other lights had gone out, he tried in his desperation to find some glimmer of light from inside himself.

He sat for some long and unknown time, as the darkness seemed to press in on him, closer and closer; till there came a moment when it was all just too much, and at that moment it seemed that something broke in him. And as it broke, he felt then a sharp pain that went right through him; but to his surprise it was not the sort of pain that had accompanied his feelings of misery; it was not the sort of pain he had been feeling before at all. This pain only lasted a brief moment, and it was a little like jumping into cold water. It was a wholesome sort of pain, and when it was gone it seemed that it was the frail shell of his pride and fear that had broken. He felt light, and ever so fresh. He opened his eyes, as if for the first time, as something strong and sure from deep inside him rose to greet the darkness. He had found a light from inside himself, and that was stronger than any other light.

Macky and Es meanwhile, were becoming increasingly sure that the darkness was growing heavier around them, and they had begun to feel increasingly uncomfortable. But still there was no sign of Vince, and still they walked on.

They would not have walked on, if they had not known that Vince was somewhere out in that terrible darkness, all alone and afraid. They would have turned and ran, or hid in the darkness itself – a hopeless plan but all too often a tempting one. But love, has a strength far greater than any such darkness, and so they walked on; slow and steady, and without doubt.

Soon they found that they had entered a great cavern. They knew this from the way their hushed whispers echoed in the vast space around them. They could not see the cavern for the darkness was absolute – but for two roses which led them on like trust.

But still, there was no sight of the third rose.

Where was Vince??

The question turned in Macky's mind. Not for the first time, and not for the last time.

It was not long since they had entered the cavern before the darkness had increased even more, though they had not thought that possible, and it had become even heavier too, so that it weighed down on them like a damp blanket. Macky shivered as he wondered how long it had been lingering there. Down here the light of the sun was a faraway thing, so too were the things it revealed, the colours, the sunlight, the things of the outside world. All was veiled to Macky and Es then, except of course the things that are revealed by darkness. Pride and fear – such things that are wont to hide from the light of the sun. But there is another light, that is quite beyond the light and darkness that we know. No pride nor fear can hide from it. No darkness can conceal it. Such was the light that Vince felt inside himself then; and such was the light that, in that heaviest of darknesses Macky and Es saw at last. There, up ahead of them – its petals like beads of glowing certainty – the third rose. And although the darkness pressed in on it from every side, it seemed that in fact it shone out all the more radiantly and rose-like now. Framed by its opposite, and untouched by it: it was powerless yet beyond power – and it swept away their fear, for by its light he saw clearly how fleeting and temporary the darkness, and all such problems were, in the light of its eternity.

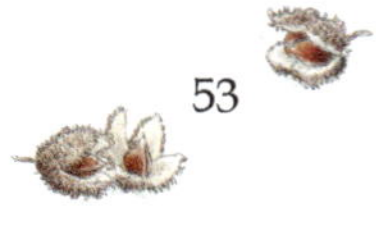

Chapter 11

Macky stooped, and gently picked up the rose. Its petals were like tissue paper and seemed so light and fragile in the heaviness of the darkness that was all around. But holding it up, the cave seemed a little lighter. And that was when Macky saw something sat on the floor of the cave, amongst the throbbing dark.

It was Vince – they had not seen him before, because he had been hidden by the cloud of darkness. It is unfortunate that one seldom does see what lies behind a cloud. But by the light of a rose one sees things clearer and now Macky's steady eyes had pierced through the cloud; right into the very middle of it, where Vince sat.

A moment passed, that seemed a lifetime, and then, Vince turned towards them, and his face lit up as he saw them.

At last Macky and Es had reached Vince, and they were together once more, in the light of the roses that shone gently in their hands. A pure white light that reminded them of the sun; of the blue sky, of the warmth of each other's company.

Vince's rose was fragile and quivering in Macky's paw, and Macky knew that even the slightest movement would cause it to break. Slowly he drew his arm towards Vince.

Slowly Vince drew his arm towards the rose. For a moment their two hands met, as Vince took the rose; and something flowed between them then that was love, and truth.

Then the rose broke, in that slightest of movements, only no, it did not break, but quite the opposite; for it seemed that the light they had so cherished in their roses now shone from inside them, only stronger. It was now a light of certainty and love, while the rose's light had been of hope. And although it broke form, and the petals wafted from their hands into the darkness – it was still a rose.

And as the petals, white as snowflakes, drifted apart from one another, it seemed that the rose was expanding, so that soon it filled the whole of the cave with its pure white light.

Vince had never before seen anything so beautiful or strong. And never before had he felt so truly beautiful and strong himself.

They were in the centre of darkness, but there they had found light.

There they had seen behind the greatest sorrow, a bottomless joy. And there they saw that every evil could be turned to a far greater good.

There was a long and joyful pause, like a concert that has ended without clapping. Then they turned to follow the gentle stream of cool air which had begun to waft through the cavern. Through another passage it wound its way, up and up – leading them at last, out of the cave.

Chapter 12

The Smoothling had just climbed above a thick band of mist, through which a distant light seeped in a golden haze. It had hung about him in its many mirrors, which expanded the sky to the vastest and most light filled cathedral, and it had been keeping him company for most of his ascent with its impenetrable silent whiteness, in which one could have heard a pebble drop all the way back down in the village.

Now, at last, the weary Smoothling had climbed so high that he had poked his head above it, and his head was shortly followed by his shoulders, legs, and finally bog-sodden toes.

He stood on an island, closer to the sky than earth. A tiny drop of stone, in a sea of clouds lapping and coiling about the mountain and all the lands below him.

Above him he saw the last stretches of the mountain filing up to the now not so distant top of the world, and around it a small company of wispy clouds; and above it a relentless sky that seemed much closer and vaster than it had ever seemed to the Smoothling before.

Now the summit beckoned him on all the more and though he was exhausted his feet seemed to grow an extra bounce in them. And so at last he scrambled up the last inches of scree and seated himself with content on the tower of wobbly blocks, which made up the summit.

'At last!' He said.

'The top of the world.'

He sat a while longer, and it seemed he had left his thoughts and worries one by one down in the mists below. In fact it did not even occur to him to think at all. For a moment, or more, he simply sat and observed that place he had arrived in. Absorbing the whole wide world which lay before him, and feeling as though his spirit had been set free from the chains of gravity, and now darted among the clouds above him.

At last the mist unrolled like a great curtain, and far below him the Smoothling now saw the city; nestled like a tiny cluster of glowing ants between the huge giants of the mountains.

This was a place above it all; closer to the mighty worlds of cloud, and light, than the frail pile of rock, that seemed ever to be melting from beneath his feet. As a gateway it seemed, between the lands below and above; an island that housed the light of the sun in many subtle tones that tinged the clouds, who carried these messages from the sun in many silver drops.

The longer the Smoothling sat in this land of light the more he got used to the perspective that one gets at the top of the world, so that soon he began to forget how one sees from the depths of a cluttered valley like Sgurr Mòr.

From here, he found it hard to believe how all those tiny little people, in their tiny little houses, in that tiny little town – could think they were so very great and in control – from here Sgurr Mòr and all its ways looked but as feeble and fragile as a broken eggshell on a wave.

But then he remembered how it was to think from the depths of a valley and he understood. He understood that down there the Smoothlings' creation of Sgurr Mòr was so big and so close around them that they thought it and all its ways were so very big; while the mountains, seemed so small and irrelevant. This of course was only because the town was very near and the mountains were very far, but the Smoothlings could not see it so – such was their enchantment.

Suddenly the Smoothling saw that this enchantment had caused the Smoothlings to be just like the Mackys of the Beechwood! For although outwardly they seemed so very different, and the

Smoothling had always remembered the Mackys of the Beechwood to be so queer and alien from *his* people, he saw now that really, on the inside they seemed to be under a very similar enchantment. The Smoothling now saw that this was really a very old enchantment, except that he had only been able to notice it after his travels with Macky, on which he became a little less enchanted himself. For the Smoothling now understood that he too had been under its illusion, and not so long ago either; for he remembered now how his worries about it all had been so terribly out of proportion. How he had taken every shadow for a wicked enchanter, every sound for a sinister plot.

Time stretched on and on in the now, so that now seemed eternal in a way it tends to in places like the top of the world.

The Smoothling watched the hustle bustle of the distant lights of the village a while longer, before at last asking into the night:

'But who is the enchanter??'

The question sounded out like a bell; loud and sure in the silence of his mind.

No one in particular answered, but the answer came to him then, dropped from a great purple cloud in the first drop of rain. It landed on his palm – a little mirror in which, as he gazed into its tiny reflection, he saw a tiny little version of the whole wide world which lay stretched out beneath him.

I feel much alike to this raindrop, realized the Smoothling then, tiny and individual; yet inside me the entire world is living so that I don't feel alone at all, but both entirely unique and one at once.

And so the Smoothling and the raindrop sat a while longer, together at the highest point of the world, and both felt very glad for each other's company.

Until at last the raindrop melted into the Smoothling's skin.

Then slowly many more rain drops came down to join him, and when he looked up at the sky he saw above him that the beautiful deep purple cloud had begun to dance; shrinking and changing its shape like a winged dervish, as it emptied itself upon him. And then the Smoothling saw that together all those little raindrops had formed their own unique cloud, and he understood that if any raindrop changed or fell, it would be a slightly different cloud.

Smoothlings are very alike to rain drops, he thought again.

And so it was that the answer came to him. Of course, it is *themselves* who are the enchanters! The Smoothlings themselves! They are both enchanted and enchanters. His mind was clear now of the giants and ogres that his fear had conjured. The enchanter he saw plainly now – just as ugly as before – but understood now, it had shrunk into its rightful place. And he knew then too, that he should have had more kindness for the wicked and terrifying enchanter whom he had suspected – for he himself had been one!

The rain stopped. The sun grew warmer; and the raindrops turned to steam on his skin as they wafted to the clouds once more.

'Nothing can hide from the top of the world...'

Macky's words echoed in the Smoothling's mind – for while he had sat, immersed in its presence, engulfed in its magnificent spirit; it had seemed that the all-seeing eyes of this land of cloud and light, had pierced right through him; to the very depths of the world inside him, where it had seen him truly and drawn him forth so, along with the deepest secrets, that few saw apart from its steady eyes. Deep, deep from within him, it had drawn them out, until he saw for himself the answers to his questions that had lain so long unseen inside himself.

The Smoothling sat but a moment longer, then, getting up he waved goodbye and set off back down the mountain.

He did not need to be at the top of the world anymore. Now he was ready to go home.

He was eager and springy, and if he had been fast going up the mountain he was even faster going down, for his fear of the enchanter had now evaporated completely, leaving him light and free and clear, and his love for the other Smoothlings welled up inside him, stronger than ever for their absence and his clarity; and it gave him great hope to know that if they can fix this enchantment they will have cured not only the enchanted but enchanter as well!

Part Four

Chapter 13

From a small hole in the ground, just outside the city of Sgurr Mòr, three figures could be seen emerging – two small, and one large and furry – rising to greet the bright sky; which called forth devotion in its endless blue.

Macky and the two children had been shown the entrance to the cave and they were all very glad to see daylight again. They thought that everything looked very much more beautiful than it had before they had gone into the cave.

Macky looked about him at the place in which he had arrived. He stood in a large hanging valley high above the waterfall around which many peaks pointed to the sky emphasizing its beauty, while they poured their fine harvest of rainwater down into a great loch, through many white veins. And there in front of him – frail, yet sickeningly proud, lay the home of the Smoothlings: the city of Sgurr Mòr.

Behind him, in the far distance, stood the mightiest mountain he had ever seen. It towered right up until it almost touched the sun, and in fact it seemed to have been singed by it – for around its black summit that was all filed to a pinpoint, were a few lonely puffs of smoke; all radiant and infused with light.

'The top of the world,' he whispered in awe. And although Macky had never seen it before, he had always felt its presence; a potent mind that no one could hide from, eyes that watched over the world – bringing messages from the stars, the sun and the lofty clouds.

Es And Vince watched the mountain too, but they were not looking at the lofty peak now, for as their eyes had adjusted to the sun, they noticed that a speck of rock seemed to be moving slowly down the mountain, having detached from its vast granite flanks. But as it drew nearer they saw that in fact it wasn't a rock, but the Smoothling on his way back from the top of the world!

The Smoothling was very surprised to see Macky and his two children up by the city; and not by the waterfall – but they had so many exciting things to talk about, and he was in such a good mood after his trip to the top of the world that he completely forgot that he had expected them to be kept 'safe and sound', and indeed he had also forgotten that he thought they *would* be safer kept away from such adventures. There was much excited telling of stories, and then when the moon rose with a faithful following of planets, Macky said to the Smoothling, 'You helped me to see with my heart little Smoothling, all that time ago, and now I would like to help your Smoothling friends to see with theirs, too.' 'Come, let's go to the city.'

Now, as they approached the city, Macky saw that it was a very queer place indeed. Not the sort of place you'd expect people in colourful cladding to live in – for it was very drab and much in need of flowers and trees. It was not at all homely and the houses couldn't have been more different from the Beechwood homes, thought Macky with a hint of his old Beechwood reminiscing. They towered up like fangs that were too tall and not at all laughing, and all through its stuffy streets, the people plodded on – sad, serious and full of fear. They were caught up in their thoughts that bounced and echoed about them – a delirious retinue of fantasies. To sum it up, it was not at all a natural place to live. But, this was not a weight on Macky and his company, for they carried with them all the truth to be found in the wilds, and all the joy and zest of bringing it to where it was so needed; Sgurr Mòr.

Now, as Macky had been expecting, when he entered the town the Smoothlings did not see him at all, keeping their heads to the ground despite the loud clicking noise that his claws made on the cobbles. But, even so, as Macky and his companions shuffled in, the city became a little more beautiful than it had been before. The people seemed to wake a little as they passed, their droopy heads rising to the sun. Curtains were drawn which hadn't been drawn for far too long. The shadows began to seem friendlier.

All these changes were of course subtle, but Macky knew that even the subtlest change in one person affects all things, and the Smoothling never forgot the purple cloud that danced like a dervish, and how Smoothlings were, very much alike to raindrops; and so, they persevered.

As the days and months went by, Macky brought more and more joy to the Smoothlings. He brought them things of the world that lay outside theirs, the world that they had forgotten *was in fact also* theirs; he brought them things of nature.

Sometimes he would catch sunlight and guide it through their windows. Or perhaps he would catch the laughter of the wind or the strength of the sea and spread it through their troubled atmosphere. Sometimes simply his presence would warm them, for that was *his* nature.

They needed nature, these Smoothlings, and there was no one better to bring it back to them than Macky; he had lived and learned from the world and all nature. He had learnt the secrets of such things as the wind and the waves. He had watched them long, holding back nothing but his judgments; and so he had learnt. In fact Macky was now quite simply himself, and what had once been a clamshell brain now seemed to encompass the whole of the wilds. The crashing of the waves and the crackling of the fire caught in the autumn leaves. The low rushing winds which combed the whiting hair of the moors, the dancing paths that the birds took and their feathers, which sliced the air leaving no stain. Macky knew what the too often forgotten grains of sand had seen. He knew how once they'd stood as the tall and echoing bones of cliffs, standing between the sea and sky. He had felt love throbbing through his heart, pure and unstained by desire; and he knew that what the Smoothlings searched for around them in their frantic hurrying would never be found in such a way – for it could only be such nature that they searched for, whether they knew it or not. And well, that had to be found in quite a different way.

To begin with, the Smoothlings seldom noticed what he brought them, but sometimes a hope like a sunrise in winter would light up on their faces and a realization would pass through their minds – a realization of something that only their hearts could see...

Slowly the very beginning of a gateway was opening in their minds, a gateway that led to their hearts and a world that lay deep inside themselves and everything of nature. A world they knew well in their hearts but one which their minds had not seen much more than the mantle of dust that lay upon it – just as Macky once saw not much more than beechnuts and bannocks.

Chapter 14

As time went by, the streets grew ever more alive with laughter, and soon great coloured kites began to appear flying high over the hills, and the loch was more and more often alive with the contented bobbing of boats. Spring had turned to summer and at last midsummer hung ripe in the air. And on that wonderfully sunny day for the first time in a great many years, there were at last no heads hung down; because for once no one was worrying themselves with what they could gain, but were rather taking joy in what they could give, and so as they gathered together, out on the silver beaches by the loch, they played and laughed and ate lots of honey from a big pot; for once not even caring how sticky they got. And the laughter that had been all too long in coming to them opened their minds and began to burn away their enchantment in a way that only laughter can.

And so came a long-awaited moment, when the Smoothlings – feeling so unusually brave and relaxed – looked out of themselves to see their fellow Smoothlings and the world around them, as if for the first time. And in fact, as they did, they also looked out to see two furry paws with long nails lifting the honey pot and emptying it swiftly!

The honey was of course being consumed by a very merry Macky, (who had been taking advantage of not being seen) a creature the likes of which they had never seen and could never have imagined, which made it all the more real now that they did see it!

The Smoothlings who were by now getting quite at ease in themselves, shrieked with delight when they saw the kindly creature, who would have been red in the face if he hadn't been so pleased that they had at last seen him.

He said something then about somebody maybe helping him get his paw free, which seemed to have got stuck in the pot. But whatever his words were, they came out in a muffle all drowned out by a mouth full of honey, and the Smoothlings' delighted shrieks and chatter.

Now after the midsummer party had chased the night right past the next day and the day after that, the people lay in the meadow exhausted in a contented sort of way. And now that they had begun to get used to the idea of a 'Macky' and all the newness that such a creature brought with it, they found themselves becoming rather curious about his country, his story and his people.

They imagined that Macky's country must be full of 'heroes' like him, but Macky told them that the Beechwood was actually full of exceptionally *ordinary* beings (if there can be such a thing) and that really they were under an enchantment too, much like the one that the Smoothlings had been under. He told them that he had only changed himself when he had gone on an *adventure*.

'When you go on an adventure you set out to wander along the edges of life, sharpening them, and refining life's form in your mind as you go.'

'To be able to see life's form' said Macky, 'you must step out of what comforts you and what you know, and when you do you must not close your eyes and walk blindly, for you must see it – and feel its full force thrumming through you; its thin edges beneath your feet.'

'And no matter how difficult it gets' he added, 'remember to keep up courage, for it is a certainty born out of love that keeps one balancing along those fine edges of life.'

'But indeed though my country is not one full of "heroes", it is true that ordinary, flawed people like you and I, have taught me much more than I could have learnt if I had been surrounded only by wise people!'

Some of the Smoothlings weren't quite sure whether to take this as a compliment or not, and they shuffled awkwardly in their seats.

And although they had very much liked the idea of visiting a country full of wise Mackys, and of perhaps even gaining some of that wisdom for themselves, they were rather shocked at the prospect of *adventures.* 'Isn't it dangerous!??' They demanded.

But Macky could only answer 'No more dangerous than Sgurr Mòr …' Then after a pause he added, 'everywhere is dangerous without enough courage or love.'

But the Smoothlings were by no means satisfied by this. 'What if we get lost??' they fretted, 'what if we get hurt??'

But Macky would simply answer, 'what if you don't.' And after many more 'what ifs' and many more fantastic stories of Macky's adventures, a long sleeping passion began to re-awaken in the Smoothlings' hearts. Until it finally dawned on them that they actually wanted an adventure themselves, and in fact what they chiefly wanted was to help the enchanted Mackys of the Beechwood. They slowly began to realize how for many a year they had been in a dream-like enchantment, and now a great freedom filled their lungs, as they looked with a growing excitement towards the unknown – and their adventure. And so they decided that when autumn came they would set off for their adventure; for that is the time of year when the coming of the cold and dark prompts you to kindle a fire inside yourself. Nature's outer shell crumbles to the dust of earth once more, and from its shell, a life is born that shines out as joyfully as the autumn leaves.

Chapter 15

Macky sat on the cusp of the great hanging valley that surrounded Sgurr Mòr. He was watching the point where the water gushed over the edge of the cliffs, and what had seemed a quiet stream showed its raw power as it transformed in an instant into the dragon that spat with power and life: the dragon, of whom Macky had grown so fond; and with whom he had shared so much time, so many jokes and so many thoughts.

Macky watched it roar and smoke as it thundered into the waiting rocks, dizzyingly far below him. As he watched, a single golden leaf spiralled slowly through the breath of the waterfall; and came gently to rest on his patch of moss – that patch that he always liked to sit on best.

Autumn was here, and it was time to take the Smoothlings on their adventure. Macky knew he would never again sit on that patch of moss in the tranquility of the spray. But he also knew that he had not come to say goodbye. For he loved this place and knew that it would always be lodged deep in his heart: a quiet yet thunderous place of tranquility held within him, no matter where his journey took him.

And so with those thoughts, Macky turned to fetch the Smoothlings for their adventure.

A great buzz of excitement hovered about the city. The Smoothlings were now ready to set off, their bags were packed and their feet itching. But when Macky saw their bags he told them to leave them behind. 'You won't be needing them!' he exclaimed confidently. And so with some excitement, along with some apprehension they set off.

They took the same route through the caves, as Macky and the children had taken on their way, and even though Macky's mind had been growing ever more flexible, his legs had grown even *less* flexible in his old age.

The Smoothlings were very afraid when they found out that they were going into a cave, However, Macky reminded them that this too would pass – for all troubles do.

Once out of the caves, they arrived in the gaping light of the wild lands beyond, and a fresh blue day greeted them with a sprightly breeze. The Smoothlings could now hardly help from galloping out into the moors!

As their journey went on over mountain and moor and valley they began to feel stronger and braver, and ever more themselves; and as they did, they began to stop mistaking themselves and each other for the things they did, or thought or felt.

And so, for many days and nights, weeks and months, the little gathering wandered through the moors, ever following the winding stream, which meandered down towards the Beechwood. And

soon they began to feel rather at home in the wilds, and their minds became as clear as the water they were drinking.

Every now and then, Macky would stop in his tracks, close his eyes and take a great sniff of the air, then wander slowly on. He knew this landscape well, and now and again he thought he caught the scent of beechnuts on the wind, or heard, perhaps, the rustle of distant tree top branches.

It stirred something in his heart; a feeling similar to the tugging, swelling feeling that he had felt long ago – when a little Smoothling had first cried in his arms.

Their journey went on.

The winds grew colder.

And at times it all seemed impossible. But Macky encouraged them that it wasn't, because if you are doing what feels right, nothing is impossible, if you have enough certainty and determination. And so they found a way through whatever obstacle had temporarily dampened their spirits.

At last as winter drew around them, and the first snows had begun to lay their silent sparkling blanket upon the earth, the Beechwood came into view – a gently swaying crowd of waiting beech trees, badgers, and bannocks.

They were almost back.

Part Five

Chapter 16

When Macky and his company finally arrived at the Beechwood they were welcomed quite rudely by the back of 'The End' sign. It had been freshly painted with neat red paint, as it was at the beginning of every winter – quite by routine. The beech trees still swayed in a listless demotivated wind, the path from 'The End' sign was still well kept and puddle free.

Despite all the changes that had happened in Macky and the Smoothlings, here, all still seemed to be the same – or almost, as Macky was soon to find out.

Now in the moment that Macky had first seen 'The End' sign it had seemed so absurd to him that he hadn't been able to help himself from plucking it triumphantly from the ground whilst bursting out in laughter, so that he toppled over and began to roll around in the muddy puddles that had surrounded it. This was a very funny sight especially because it was a real struggle for him to get back up again, and so the Smoothlings all laughed and cheered and began to roll around too, causing quite a racket.

Now this sudden and unusual commotion aroused the Beechwood in an instant, and along came rushing a great crowd of Mackys, including Macky's mother, Doctor Droon, various other important Beechwood figures, and a couple of curious badgers.

Of course *they* only saw one very cheeky and muddy looking Macky, and not the long trail of very amused and amazed looking Smoothlings, who had got quite a shock at seeing Mackys who behaved so differently to the Macky they knew! For the Beechwood residents now stood in a neat semi-circle around the muddy Macky, grumbling and wagging their fingers at him in an exceptionally formal manner.

'So you're back' Macky's mother scolded him, 'and about time too. We're beginning to have quite enough of these unusual going-ons,' she said sternly, with a tremor in her voice.

'Your little disappearance trick has caused quite an unnecessary and dangerous fuss that hasn't been seen here in the Beechwood in all my days!' Her voice was now rising to a squeak and with a fright she realized that she too was making quite an unusual fuss!

And that was when Macky first realized that something *had* changed.

For it came out then that since Macky's disappearance, his uncle who had always been considered eccentric, (though only by Beechwood standards) had started writing a *history* book. And due to this all sorts of open-minded theories had been born as to where Macky had gone, which as you can imagine quite upset the older generation of Mackys; who, when they heard about the history book had said things like: 'don't be absurd.'

'What's the world coming to?'

'Never in a million beech trees!' and all the other commonly regurgitated Beechwood proverbs that spread such comfort about the place that it was more a place of butter than toast.

'You have to be careful,' said Doctor Droon with all his usual authority, 'doing strange and unusual things; it can drive one mad!'

And that's why we are so *normal*!' the crowd proudly chirped in. 'You never know where the unknown might lead, that's why there is no unknown in the Beechwood!' They quoted in unison.

Now as the Mackys retreated away from the edge of the Beechwood as fast as possible without losing their dignity, Macky's uncle shouldered his way through the crowd towards Macky. His chest was so puffed out with pride that the buttons of his grand purple waistcoat had burst right off, and he took Macky by the hand exactly as he sometimes had when Macky had won the 'how many beechnuts in a jar' competition and such like... Although he was not so proud of Macky himself now, but proud more because he thought that Macky's claim that he had in fact been out of the wood, proved his history book right.

Actually his history was an incredibly limited, and warped version of Macky's real story, stating quite simply that:

'Macky had got lost outside the Beechwood – as naturally you would – but while stumbling about aimlessly he had found, quite by chance, that there *was* a world beyond the Beechwood, which was of course a beech wood too, containing the usual size and form of beech tree, a population of badgers, and of course squirrels as well, only *this* Beechwood was constantly covered in such a thick fog that the beech trees could not easily be seen.

He suspected that spending such time in a world full of fog would most likely have effected Macky's psychology, and that during his time out he may have come up with all sorts of backward fantasies which would seem so bizarre to logical Beechwood thinking that they would be incomprehensible to the Beechwood mind, and therefore the Mackys should be rather on their guard for his return, in case he talked about anything unordinary.

This snippet of information that had now wormed its way into the Beechwood culture was largely taken for nonsense – because everyone knew that there was 'nothing' past 'The End' sign – and the more civilised of Mackys seemed to have come to the long-winded conclusion that actually Macky had taken up residence with the badgers (which the badgers all denied profusely).

But there was also a group of Mackys looking for a change though largely for their own benefit, who developed the technique called 'Peering', which was their method, of standing at 'The End' sign and trying to peer out in order to draw conclusions about it without actually going out of the wood. And so a certain obsession about the 'world outside the Beechwood' was born amongst these Mackys, and they had soon given birth to all sorts of crazy theories that drove the older generation quite mad. Such as the one that stated that actually Macky had found a world in which the beech trees were just very very small and couldn't be seen to the untrained eye; or the theory that suggested that it was a world where squirrels had no fur, because the nothingness was so warm, and that was where the well circulated myth of 'Smoothlings' came from.

There was another theory that believed that this 'Outside World' was the source of all joy because there was an unlimited amount of beechnuts there.

These theories may seem bizarre now that you have heard a little about the world outside the Beechwood, but if you or I had also lived in the Beechwood all our lives, perhaps we too might have had such beliefs!

For you see when they peered out they were of course only able to see what by chance fell into their Beechwood logic – perhaps, for example they did see a real sprig of heather, but the only plants they could comprehend, were beech trees. Or maybe they even saw a Smoothling but believed it to be a squirrel, for squirrels were all they knew. Or a beechnut could have blown out in the wind, but seeing only it, they assumed that it was all there was...

Such is the danger of Beechwood logic.

Chapter 17

For many weeks and months the Smoothlings and the Mackys lived alongside one another. The Smoothlings wandered the moors and woods, quite contentedly, as they had now grown quite comfortable in wild places, away from their Smoothling houses. But sometimes on the colder days they sneaked into the Beechwood houses inside which the Mackys spent most of the winter. They always hoped that they might at last be seen.

But time and time again they were taken only for a breeze; or perhaps the patter of a passing squirrel.

Until at last there came one bleak midwinters day, when something changed. It was the day on which by tradition, everyone gave presents to one another.

Outside the snow fell thick and clean, laying a great calm over the land. The snow stuck to the forest floor faster than any number of Mackys could clear the path; soon covering trees and bushes and every Macky home in its thick white coat so that you really couldn't have told the difference between tree or home or bush, for they all just looked like obscure dollops of cream and not at all the familiar shapes they had previously been.

Because of this unfamiliarity the Mackys would never normally have gone out on such a day; but today, every single one of them was out. This was because they had to find the usual presents to give to their family and friends, and due to their nature, they didn't have the imagination to look for other sorts of presents instead. For you see the presents were never much of a surprise in the Beechwood. They were actually *always* beechnuts – because it would have been very antisocial to display signs of imagination through finding an alternative present. And, because of course the Mackys hated surprises, though they did love presents very much, and so they had found a sort of a compromise.

But that day the beechnuts were all buried very deeply beneath the snow and they soon found themselves roaming further and further towards the edges of the wood in search of them. Now as they did they naturally fell into each other's tracks, for it was easier for their short shuffling legs which did not do at all well in snow. And soon they found that they had formed one big and very concerned group, which jostled and grumbled clumsily digging itself deeper into the snow.

Around them the wind picked up, whisking the snow into dancing ghosts and causing icicles to grow on their long, thick fur. The miserable group soon begun to realize that they were lost; the tracks had now totally disappeared and since they had all opted for *following* each other's tracks there was no one to set *new* tracks, and so they consented miserably to being snowed in. Such a snow had never before been seen in the Beechwood's mild climate, nor such a gale as the one that howled that day – sending the snow and hail into an endless horizontal stream that pierced their faces, and roused them to a reluctant and painful awakening.

The day was growing dark.

Macky creatures seldom go out in the dark.

Their paws were cold, and believe it or not they were beginning to have an adventure in their very own Beechwood!...

Suddenly lightning flashed and thunder bellowed and in that brief moment of light, they saw just a little way ahead of them, a trail! There was much jostling, grumbling and muttering but they followed it none-the-less because it was the only thing that they could do.

It wasn't long after they began to follow the track that they saw in the distance, stark against the white of the snow, a figure with thick brown fur shuffling slowly by. It was carrying a small light that still seemed to be shining despite the winds. It was a glowing warmth against the cold.

Slowly it shuffled on.

Quickly they hurried after it.

The beech trees grew sparser around them.

The wind grew stronger.

But although the gale was only getting worse and the wildness only closer, a strange thing happened to the Mackys then, as they shuffled after the light. For as the gale worsened the light became all the more of a comfort to them, and though on the outside it became dimmed by the darkening storm, it grew in their hearts; from a glimmer of hope, to an ever growing certainty, and soon it was not just a need for warmth that drew them to it but rather there was something of a deeper comfort that they had found in it, which seemed to fill them, till they forgot about their cold toes, and really nothing seemed so bad anymore, as they began even to look upon the wilds with joy. For there is only so much of a storm that such

Mackys are able to cope with, and after that, well, they will get to a point when need draws them to see more in light than warmth. Their fear will begin to melt in the light, and they will feel a courage in their hearts, that no fear could have ever driven back; and, they may not even worry when they pass beyond the shade of the last beech trees...

Chapter 18

There was once a place here, at the edge of the wood, where a sign said that this was 'The End.' There was once a place here, at the edge of the wood, where safety ended and adventure began. Where the world one knew became the unknown. Where there was a bridge between love and fear.

But now the sign was gone, and it seemed that the line had become somewhat blurred. Too many hearts that now roamed the Beechwood, had also roamed the world outside. The bridge had grown wider, and now as the group of Mackys followed the glow in the gale, love had grown stronger than fear.

They had crossed the bridge though they did not know it, at the moment that the light had given them courage to go out into the gale rather than turn in in despair.

Up ahead of them, the light had stopped moving and was growing closer as they padded after it. As it did they thought they saw, behind the curtain of snow and wind, that the light now seemed to shine on more than one glowing figure. And as they drew nearer still, they could not be mistaken that a group of the most unusual looking figures were huddled around the light.

Now despite the howling of the wind there was a great silence. The sort of silence that only the white of the snow can bring.

The silence enveloped them, and from its very centre they began to hear music, a rich sweet music that was the tinkling of bells and the deep sound of the cello at once; music that was both laughing and rejoicing, and swelling with passion and love, it was a music that came from silence. Beechwood logic had always thought of white as nothing. But now how colourful and joyful the white seemed; and the 'nothing'!

That is a true present, thought the Smoothling as he made room around the light for the Mackys.

To realize a friend in something you had always denied; to be seen and to see.

And that indeed was the first true midwinter celebration that had happened for a very long time in the Beechwood.

The Mackys were on the beginning of a journey – a long journey, and a difficult one. It was a journey that followed a path, a greatly subtle path on which they could not see more than a couple of steps ahead – due to the fog, Macky's uncle still claimed.

But, despite its challenging ways, that were most certainly full of surprises, it was a path that was full of joy too, and it welcomed them, for deep inside their hearts they welcomed it, too. Like raindrops, they must walk this path – in clouds, in streams, and in the many mirrors of fog.

The Mackys took to the Smoothlings at once, and the days and months and years to follow were ones of much excitement, as Macky after Macky began to look on the world with new eyes. And after a sudden mass bout of claustrophobia and itchy feet, for which there was no cure except for adventure, the Mackys along with their new guides and dear friends the Smoothlings, started to explore the world outside the Beechwood. The houses were handed over to the badgers, and soon a great many adventures were had, and though not all of the Smoothlings and Mackys went on adventures up mountains and across the sea and things of that sort, each had an adventure of his own kind – each experienced something new and uncomfortable and began to learn from it.

Es and Vince, had certainly not yet had enough of adventures, so they too had gone out with the other Smoothlings and Mackys

Outside the Beechwood

to explore the world outside the Beechwood. And so Macky soon found himself quite alone again with the Smoothling, in the quiet of the now largely deserted Beechwood, which had begun to feel much more natural since the Mackys had finally neglected its finicky 'maintenance'. He and the Smoothling would have been seen then swinging gently in Macky's stripy red hammock in which they were curled. Macky felt quite tired now, but it was a very contented sort of tired that he felt. He had been on so many adventures, and had so much fun; he had learnt a great many things, and though he had so very much still to learn, he knew that what he had not yet learnt he would one day learn. Because, as he often quoted, 'All's well that ends well, and if all's not well, its not the end!'

And so he took to his hammock to look back on it all, and to rest before his next journey – a very different sort of journey.

We have one more journey to do together, Macky could have been heard saying to the Smoothling, who's eyelids were already closing...

Chapter 19

All was quiet in the Beechwood but for the crackle of the dying fire.

The hammock creaked.

The moon rose huge and orange; and Macky's front paw drooped from the hammock as he and the Smoothling fell to a deep and contented sleep.

A sleep that was both deeper and more contented than the night sky itself – and so at last the night lifted its veil to them, and welcomed them back.

The vast expanses opened up.

The colours shone.

And the stars took them in their silvery hands to teach them at last their secrets.

Macky and the Smoothling had learnt what they had needed to learn at that time on the earth.

It was now time for their next adventure.